Disney

My Very First
Encyclopedia
with Winnie the Pooh and Friends

ANIMALS

p

This is a Parragon book
This edition published in 2006
Parragon
Queen Street House
4 Queen Street
Bath, BA1 1HE, UK

ISBN 1-40546-579-4
Printed in Malaysia

Hello!
We're looking
for animals!

Come along with us and you'll meet all kinds of animals!

You'll meet big animals and small animals,
baby animals and grown-up animals,
noisy animals and quiet animals.

You'll meet a lot of animals covered with fur.
And you'll meet animals covered with feathers.

Animals can squeak, purr, coo, and hiss.
And animals can run, crawl, hop, fly, and swim.

Some animals have wings, some have fins,
and some have lots of legs.

Come along! Help us look for all kinds of animals!

Parent's Note

This comprehensive encyclopedia about the world of animals is specially designed for the active preschool learner. Winnie the Pooh and his friends will introduce your child to the wide variety of creatures that exist inside and outside the Hundred-Acre Wood. Pooh and his pals will gently encourage your young discoverers to make real-life connections between the animals in this book and themselves. The chapters of this book are organized to help young children learn how to recognize the things animals have in common with one another.

Throughout this book, children will find their favourite characters from the Hundred-Acre Wood on hand to guide them through the various sections. Each character brings a unique voice to the world of amazing discovery that's about to unfold.

Pooh shares his sense of wonder and explorations of the world of animals throughout the book.

Tigger introduces amazing facts about some pretty Tiggerific elements of animals.

Piglet invites children to apply their newfound knowledge about animals with beautifully illustrated look-and-find pages.

Roo asks Kanga simple questions about animals and discovers some fascinating facts.

What's inside?

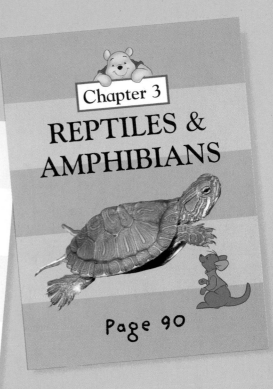

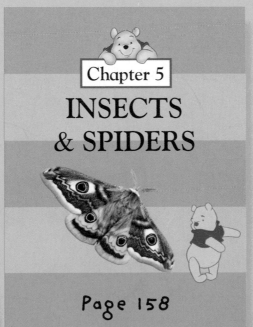

Chapter 1

MAMMALS

Pooh Wonders . . .

Pooh was out walking when he heard a familiar sound: BOING! BOING! BOING!

"Hello, Tigger," Pooh greeted his friend as Tigger bounced him over.

"Hello, Pooh!" Tigger cried.

Pooh sat up and brushed himself off. "Oh, look, Tigger," he said. "You've got some fur on me. It's nice and soft."

"Of course!" Tigger exclaimed. "All Tiggers have nice, soft fur." He poked Pooh in the tummy. "Poohs do, too."

"Oh, yes," Pooh agreed. "Does that mean a pooh bear is a sort of tigger? Or that a tigger is a sort of pooh bear?"

"I don't know, Pooh. But I think we'd better find out."

Pooh walked, and Tigger bounced to Rabbit's house.

"Hello, Rabbit!" Tigger stopped in mid-bounce on Rabbit's tummy. "Rabbit!" he cried. "You have nice, soft fur, too!"

Pooh gasped. "Does that mean rabbits are a sort of pooh bear or tigger?"

"Don't be silly. We're all mammals – that's why we all have fur," said Rabbit.

"Mamminals?" Pooh said.

"Mammals," Rabbit corrected. "That's a sort of animal that has fur."

"Well," Pooh said thoughtfully. "I expect most mamminals also like honey. Perhaps we should all go inside and have a smackerel now!"

"Come on, let's meet some mammals!"

5

A lion is a mammal that lives in the wild.

A pig is a mammal that lives on a farm.

"Owl, what is a mammal?"

A mammal is an animal.
All of these animals are mammals.
Mammals can be big or small,
striped or spotted.
They can be brown, white,
black, or even red.

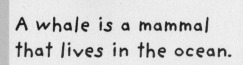

A whale is a mammal that lives in the ocean.

You are
a mammal, too!

A rabbit is
a mammal
with big ears.

"What makes an animal a mammal?"

Mammals have hair or fur.
- Mammals take good care of their babies.
- Mammal babies drink their mother's milk.

Guess what? You're a mammal, too!

An orangutan is a mammal that has fingers and toes.

A polar bear is a mammal that lives in the North Pole.

7

Hello, Boys and Girls!

"My, my, Piglet. I believe Christopher Robin is a mammal, too!"

Just Born!

Look at the baby! She's a few weeks old. Like all mammals, she grew inside her mummy until she was born. She also has lots of hair as do some mammals. What did you look like when you were born?

Growing Up!

This baby is two years old. Just like you, he had to learn how to walk. He can talk now, too. He still needs someone to take care of him. When did you learn to walk? Who takes care of you?

Boys and Girls at Home!

People are mammals that live everywhere. Some people live in houses or on boats. Some live on farms, in flats, or in huts. Where do you live?

Hello, Cat!

"Eeyore, can you hear that cat purring?
That means she is happy."
"Must be nice. I wouldn't know."

Just Born!

Look at all these tiny kittens!
They are just a few days old.
They cannot see or hear yet.
They are sleeping. When they
wake up, they will drink their
mummy's milk.

Growing Up!

Now the kittens are four weeks old.
But they still need their mummy. She licks
them to keep them clean.
Soon they will learn
to lick their paws and
clean themselves.

Cats at Home!

Cats live just about everywhere. Some live with
people, but there are many big cats that live
in the wild. Pet cats like this one need people
to feed them and care for them.

Hello, Dog!

"Eeyore, maybe that dog can fetch some sticks to rebuild your house!"

Just Born!

A baby dog is called a puppy. How many puppies do you see? These puppies are seven days old. They cannot see or hear. They drink their mummy's milk and sleep all day.

Growing Up!

Look who has grown! This puppy is four weeks old. Now it can see and hear. Soon it will grow its baby teeth. Until then, it still needs its mummy's milk to grow.

Dogs at Home!

Some dogs live with city families. Some dogs live with country families. This dog is a pet. But there are hunting dogs, police dogs, herd dogs, and fire dogs. Dogs can do many jobs!

Hello, Rabbit!

"Ah, Pooh, have you ever seen a lovelier creature?"

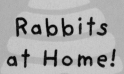

Just Born!

This mummy rabbit has five new babies. Baby rabbits are called kits. Kits do not have fur when they are born. They snuggle close to one another to stay warm in their burrow.

Growing Up!

Now look! The kits are two weeks old. They now have fur, and are able to hop. Soon they will go off on their own. In three or four months they will have their own babies!

Rabbits at Home!

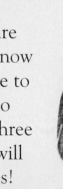

Rabbits live in many places. This one has come out of its burrow under the ground to look for food.

14

Hello, Pig!

"Pooh, I've asked my new friend to come for a visit. I think we have a lot in common!"

Just Born!

A baby pig is called a piglet. Mummy pigs have many piglets at the same time. The babies squeal and make a lot of noise. Then they line up to drink their mummy's milk.

Growing Up!

The baby pigs have grown quickly. They are only six months old. Look at how much bigger they are. Their little squeals are now big grunts.

Pigs at Home!

Pigs live on farms. They like to eat corn. And there is nothing they like more than a roll in the mud. The mud cools them down on a hot day.

It's not only cats that have spots.

Baby Tapirs from Central and South America do, too! These spots help the tapir hide in the forest. When it gets older, it will lose its spots. Then it will be all brown.

Look at this furry flyer.

It's not a bird – it's a sugar glider. These mammals don't really fly. They go from tree limb to tree limb by gliding through the air. They can glide as far as 200 feet!

Was this monkey finger-painting?

No, it looks like this, naturally. This is a mandrill. These monkeys are the largest of them all. And their faces are very colourful.

Hey, long neck!

Giraffes are the tallest of all animals. Some can grow to be 20 feet tall. That's as tall as a house!

THAT'S TIGGERIFIC!

Did you know that you have something in common with horses?

Baby horses are born without teeth . . . and so were you! Both people and horses get baby teeth, and then grown-up teeth. And that's the honest tooth!

Are you sticking your tongue out at me?

It's purple! Polar bears have purple tongues.

Hello, Horse!

"Look at it run, Eeyore!"
"It's all in the legs, Pooh.
It's all in the legs."

Just Born!

This baby horse is called a foal. It was just born. Look at its long legs! They are not very strong yet. But the foal can stand up to drink its mummy's milk.

Growing Up!

The foal is six months old. It has grown very tall. Its fur is now dark brown. And its legs are strong. It can run with its mummy.

Horses at Home!

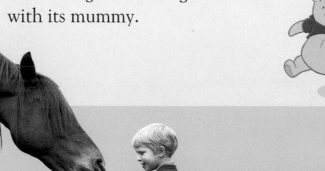

Some people have horses as pets. Their owners brush them and feed them. Horses like to eat hay. And a crunchy carrot makes a tasty treat.

Hello, Squirrel!

"See how the squirrel holds the acorn? That is a very proper way for squirrels to eat, Pooh."

Just Born!

Who are these tiny babies? They are squirrels. A baby squirrel is called an infant. Their nest is called a dray. These newborns are only a bit bigger than your thumb!

Growing Up!

The squirrels have fur. But their tails are not as bushy as they will be later on. Baby squirrels need their sleep. In a few weeks they will be playing and running all day.

Squirrels at Home!

Go, go, go! Speedy squirrels live all around trees. They come down to the ground to look for nuts and seeds. Then up they go again!

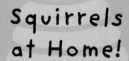

Hello, Brown Bear!

"Piglet, I suspect it takes quite a lot of honey to fill that fellow's tummy!"

Just Born!

Baby bears are called cubs. When cubs are born, they are as small as a squirrel. For now, this cub will stay inside its cosy den.

Growing Up!

It is spring now. The cubs have grown a lot. They still stay with their mummy. She keeps them safe. They follow her while they all look for sweet berries.

Brown Bears at Home!

Brown bears live in forests. They swim and fish in nearby rivers. Winter is on its way. The bears must fill their bellies with food and get ready for their winter's rest.

Hello, Porcupine!

"How do you hug a fellow like that, Piglet?"
"Very gently, Pooh."

Just Born!

This baby porcupine is called a porcupette. It was born with its quills. At first they were very soft. Now they are very sharp. Ouch!

Growing Up!

This baby is one month old. It is very curious. But it pays attention to its mummy. She shows it what to eat. Together, they look for twigs and berries.

Porcupines at Home!

See the porcupine in the tree? The forest is its home. When it sees danger, up it goes into the tree. It can climb very high. Its feet hold tightly on to the branches.

Hello, Lion!

"Do you see the hair on that lion's head, Pooh? It is called a mane."
"I hope he has a very big brush, Rabbit!"

Just Born!

A baby lion is called a cub. This cub is only two weeks old. The mummy carries the cub in her mouth. Don't worry. She is very gentle.

Growing Up!

The cubs are now six months old. Their mummy teaches them how to hunt and climb. They also rumble and tumble in the grass. That is how they play.

Lions at Home!

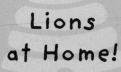

Lions live in the dry grasslands of Africa. The afternoons are very hot, too hot to hunt. So the lions rest and sleep. They will hunt at night.

Roo Wants to Know...

Are there any mammals that can fly?

Yes. Bats can fly. They also use their wings to keep warm as they sleep hanging upside down.

Do skunks really smell bad?

Only when they squirt their spray. They usually spray only when they are afraid. First they stamp their feet as a warning. But if that doesn't work, watch out.

Is a koala a bear?

No, koalas look like fuzzy bears, but they are cousins of kangaroos. Just like a kangaroo, a mummy koala carries her baby in her pouch.

Do all zebras have the same stripes?

No. Each and every zebra has its own special pattern of stripes. That helps them all find one another.

Do whales have teeth?

Some whales have teeth, and others don't. One kind of whale, the male narwhal, has a long, spiral tusk. It looks like an elephant's tusk.

Does a camel keep water in its hump?

No. Camels store fat in their humps. A camel's hump is like a rucksack filled with food when there is not enough to eat.

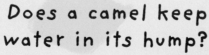

Hello, Elephant!

"It's just as well I'm not an elephant, Pooh. I'd probably lose my trunk, too."

Just Born!

A baby elephant is called a calf. This calf was inside its mummy for almost two years before being born. Its mummy helps it to its feet right away.

Growing Up!

At six months, the calf begins to eat plants. It learns what to eat by pulling food out of its mummy's mouth. But it will still nurse for three or four years.

Elephants at Home!

There are many places in the world where elephants live. They stay together in a big group called a herd. Mothers, babies, grandmothers, aunts, cousins, brothers, and sisters all live together. They take care of each other.

Hello, Giraffe!

"That giraffe has a very long neck, Piglet. It takes its food a long time to get down to its tummy."

Just Born!

A baby giraffe is called a calf. This calf was just born. It can already stand up by itself. Drinking its mummy's milk will help it grow.

Growing Up!

The calf is now a year old. It is 12 feet tall! That's twice as big as it was when it was born. It will keep growing until it is 10 years old.

Giraffes at Home!

Giraffes live in the dry grasslands of Africa. It's not easy for giraffes to drink. They must spread their legs very wide. A giraffe can drink up to four gallons of water at a time.

Hello, Tiger!

"Piglet, I believe that fellow looks like someone we know. I wonder who, though?"

Just Born!

A baby tiger is called a cub. These cubs are as tiny as newborn kittens. Their eyes and ears are still closed. But they are born knowing how to drink their mummy's milk.

Growing Up!

The cubs are now six months old. They follow their mummy everywhere. She shows them how to hunt for food. They must stay quiet. If they do not, she will snarl at them to behave.

Tigers at Home!

Some tigers live in the jungles of Asia. Their stripes and colours help them hide in the tall grass. They stay very quiet when they hunt. They walk very slowly. Then suddenly . . . they pounce!

Hello, Zebra!

"Pooh! That animal looks like a horse in striped pyjamas!"
"Then it must be time for its nap, Piglet!"

Just Born!

A baby zebra is called a foal. This newborn foal grew inside its mummy for about one year. In just one hour, it will be running right by its mummy's side.

Growing Up!

The foal is now two years old. Like you, it lives with its family. Zebras travel together in a big group called a herd. This zebra will stay with its family for its whole life.

Zebras at Home!

Zebras live in the dry grasslands of Africa. They eat lots and lots of grass. But sometimes there is no rain, and zebras get very thirsty. They will travel many miles to find water.

Hello, Orangutan!

"Pooh, look at all that long red fur!"
"It's very nice indeed, Piglet."

Just Born!

A baby orangutan is called an infant. At one week old, this infant cannot crawl yet. It clings to its mummy. She carries it everywhere. Sometimes it sucks its thumb.

Growing Up!

◄ At four months, the infant learns how to find food, and is already a good climber!

This orangutan is now six years old. It is ready to be on its own. ►

Orangutans at Home!

Orangutans live in rainforests in Asia. They stay high in the treetops. The forests are filled with fruit. That is what orangutans love to eat.

This is a sloth.

It is a very slow-moving animal. It spends most of its time hanging upside down in trees. Slow sloth. Slow sloth. Slow sloth. Try saying that three times fast . . . er, slow.

Hey, cool cat!

Tiggers love tigers. They are big, big cats. They are the biggest of all cats. They are even bigger than a Tigger.

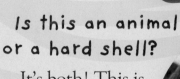

Is this an animal or a hard shell?

It's both! This is an animal called an armadillo. Look at the scales on its skin. Its skin is very strong and protects the animal.

THAT'S TIGGERIFIC!

Too big to swim? No way!

Elephants are very good swimmers. An elephant's trunk works like a snorkel. When an elephant goes underwater, its trunk stays above the water so it can breathe.

This guy slurps its food.

It's an anteater. Anteaters have long, sticky tongues. They use them to pick up ants. They think ants make a yummy meal.

Can you hear me?

Of course it can! It's a small animal, with huge ears and great hearing. This fennec fox can hear tiny insects crawling on the ground. First it hears them; then, it snaps them up!

Hello, Polar Bear!

"Pooh, I wonder if those polar bears would like some hot chocolate?"

Just Born!

A baby polar bear is called a cub. These cubs are about four months old. They still need their mummy. They snuggle up to her in the cold. She keeps them warm and safe.

Growing Up!

Young polar bears love to play. They are now a year old. Even though they are bigger, they still have things to learn from their mummy. She will teach them how to fish for food.

Polar bears at Home!

Polar bears live way up north in the frozen Arctic. But they do not mind the cold. Their thick fur keeps them warm. They swim in the cold water and walk on the ice.

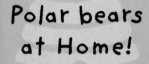

Hello, Harp Seal!

"Look at how clean that young one is, Pooh.
What do you have to say to that?"
"Well, Rabbit, perhaps it would like
a smackerel of honey!"

Just Born!

A baby seal is called a pup. Why are the pup and its mummy so close together? Its mummy is learning her baby's smell. Knowing that, she can find it anywhere.

Growing Up!

This pup is two weeks old. It is starting to get its grown-up coat. Can you see the grey fur? At one year old, this pup will be able to swim all by itself.

Harp Seals at Home!

Harp seals live on the ice. But they are not cold. They have a lot of fat under their skin. The fat helps keep them warm.

Hello, Whale!

"Look Eeyore, I can make a big splash, too!"

Just Born!

What a big baby! A baby whale is called a calf. This calf weighed 200 pounds when it was born. That is much bigger than you are now! Where was it born? Under the water!

Growing Up!

The calf stays close to its mummy. Like a human baby, it cries when it is hungry. Its mummy's milk tastes good to it. It will nurse for about two years.

Whales at Home!

Look at this whale! It dives down deep. Then up it comes! Whales dive, swim, and play in the water. But whales are mammals. So they must come up to breathe air.

48

Hello, Panda!

"Eeyore, doesn't it look like someone painted that panda's eyes and ears black?"
"Pooh, do you think I could ask to be painted something more cheerful?"

Just Born!

A baby panda is called a cub. This tiny cub was just born. It will grow 900 times bigger than it is now!

Growing Up!

At four months, the cub can walk all by itself. It crawls all over its mummy. That is how it learns to climb trees. At one year old it no longer drinks its mummy's milk. It eats yummy leaves instead.

Pandas at Home!

Pandas live in only one place in the whole world. They live in China. Their favourite food grows there. It is called bamboo. They hold bamboo in their paws and munch away.

Hello, Kangaroo!

"A pouch is a splendid place to keep a baby, Pooh. Just splendid."
"If I had a pouch, Rabbit, I would fill it with honey."

Just Born!

A baby kangaroo is called a joey. This one was no bigger than a jellybean when it was born. It will hide inside its mummy's pouch for about two months.

Growing Up!

Look who is peeking out! The joey is six months old. It is old enough to leave its mummy's pouch. But not for long! When it feels afraid, it hops right back in. Soon it will be too big for its mummy's pouch.

Kangaroos at Home!

Kangaroos live in the grasslands of Australia. It is very hot and dry there. During the day, kangaroos rest in the shade. Then at night they look for tasty plants to eat.

Look and Find with Piglet!

Now you've learnt about mammals, look at the picture and answer the questions below.

- How many mammals are on this page?

- Can you find the porcupines?

- How many rabbits are there?

- How many animals are sleeping?

- What animal is whispering in Eeyore's ear?

- What is standing on the edge of the cliff?

- Who's dreaming of antlers?

- What animal is sleeping upside down?

Chapter 2

BIRDS

Pooh Wonders . . .

Oone day Pooh noticed some robins playing tag overhead. They seemed to be having so much fun that Pooh wished he could join them.

"If only I could fly," Pooh thought.

Soon he was knocking on the door of Owl's house.

"Hello, Pooh," Owl said. "What can I do for you?"

"I came to ask you to teach me how to fly," Pooh answered.

Owl and Pooh got busy. Owl told Pooh to bend his knees. Pooh did as Owl asked.

"What next?" he said.

"Flap your wings," Owl said.

Pooh looked confused. "But Owl, I have Pooh arms, not wings! said Pooh.

Owl looked startled. "That usually works for me, Pooh. I wonder why it doesn't work for you."

Owl looked at Pooh. "I've got it," he finally said, "You're a pooh, not a bird!"

"Come on, let's meet some birds!"

A hummingbird is a bird that has a thin, long beak.

"Owl, what is a bird?"

A parrot is a bird with brightly coloured feathers.

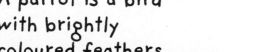

A bird is an animal.

Birds come in so many different colours! They can be blue, red, green, black, white, grey, yellow, or pink.

Most birds fly, but some just swim or walk.

Birds can sing, chirp, caw, or coo. Some birds can even talk!

An owl is a bird with big eyes.

A duck is a bird
that swims.

What makes an
animal a bird?

- All birds have feathers.
- Every bird has a beak. On some birds
  these are called bills.
- Every bird hatches from an egg.

A woodpecker
is a bird that makes
holes in trees.

A penguin is a
bird that lives
on the ice.

59

Hello, Woodpecker!

"Eeyore, listen to that woodpecker
tap on that tree!"
"I hope it doesn't tap on my house next, Pooh!"

Just Hatched!

Knock, knock! Who's there? Baby woodpeckers! They are called nestlings. Their mummy and  daddy took turns sitting on the eggs. It took 16 days for them to hatch.

Growing Up!

Hungry nestlings cry. Their mummy feeds them yummy worms. Their daddy sleeps in the nest at night. He keeps the babies safe.

Woodpeckers at Home!

Woodpeckers live in forests. They tap, tap, tap at tree bark. That makes a hole in the tree. Then they go inside and build a nest.

Hello, Owl!

"Now that's a wise and handsome fellow, Pooh!"

Just Hatched!

Who are these fuzzy babies? They are owls. Baby owls are called owlets. The fluffy baby feathers are called down. Owlets are hatched with their eyes closed.

Growing Up!

The owlets are eight weeks old now. They are losing their down and getting their grown-up feathers. It is time to fly away! The owlets have grown up. Now they can take care of themselves.

Owls at Home!

Sh-h-h! Owls fly very quietly through their forest home. Their wings move silently in the night air. That is when they search for food.

Hello, Chicken!

"Here, chick, chick, chick!"

Just Hatched!

This chick is hatching! It was snug in its egg for 21 days.
Now, little by little, it pecks away at the shell. It uses a special tooth called an egg tooth.

Growing Up!

Its egg tooth has fallen off. It doesn't need it any more! Look! Yellow, soft, and fuzzy, this chick is one week old.

The chicks have grown new feathers. What colour are they now?

Chickens at Home!

Chickens live on farms. The mummy chicken is the hen. The daddy is the cockerel. The loud cockerel calls, "Cock-a-doodle-doo!" all over the farm.

Hello, Hummingbird!

"Look, Piglet. That hummingbird is using its beak just like a straw!"

Just Hatched!

Hummingbirds are the smallest birds in the world. They begin their life in a tiny nest. The nest is soft. It is made from spiders' webs, leaves, and grass.

Growing Up!

This hummingbird is three weeks old. Soon it will have all its beautiful colours. Many people think hummingbirds look like flying rainbows.

Hummingbirds at Home!

Hummingbirds live in forests and meadows. They fly from flower to flower. Their long beaks reach inside flowers to sip the sweet nectar.

THAT'S TIGGERIFIC!

Big beak! Big beak!

A toucan's beak looks like it must be very heavy. But it isn't. Toucans' beaks are hollow inside. That makes them light-weight.

Who laid these green eggs?

An emu did. A female emu lays about seven to ten green eggs at a time.

Some birds eat bees and they don't even get stung.

These birds are called bee-eaters. They rub the bee in the ground first. This takes off the stinger. Then they gulp it down. And that's Tiggerific!

A pelican has a pouch below its beak.

The pouch can stretch . . . and stretch . . . to hold lots and lots of fish. A pelican's pouch can hold more fish than the pelican's belly can!

These geese are flying in the shape of the letter V.

They are going to a warm place for the winter. On the way, they will take turns being the leader. That's pretty Tiggerific!

Here is a little bird that doesn't fly.

It is called a kiwi. These birds live in forests in New Zealand.

Can you walk backwards?

Tiggers can. And hummingbirds are the only birds that can fly backwards. Look, there goes one now!

Hello, Duck!

"That duck is a very good swimmer, Piglet!"
"Let's go and find out, Pooh!"

Just Hatched!

This nest is hidden in the tall grass. Let's peek inside it. Look at the baby ducks! They are called ducklings. How many ducklings do you see?

Growing Up!

"Quack! Quack!" These ducklings are a few days old. They show their mummy that they can already swim. But she must keep a careful eye on them.

Ducks at Home!

Splish, splash! Ducks love the water. Can you see the duck's feet? Their feet are made for swimming. They are called webbed feet.

Hello, Pelican!

"That fellow's beak is quite a handy holdall, Pooh!"

Just Hatched!

Hello . . . Anybody down there? These pelican chicks are eating. They grab food from inside their mummy's or daddy's throat. Some pelican chicks have black feathers when they hatch. When they are older, they will turn white.

Growing Up!

The chicks are one month old. They now live in a big group with other chicks. Even looking in this big group, parents can find their own chicks.

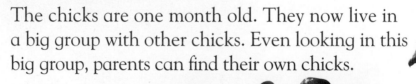

Pelicans at Home!

Pelicans live by the water. Here comes one now! Watch it swoop down and dive deep. It will catch a lot of fish in its big beak.

Hello, Penguin!

"Eeyore, that penguin looks like it's wearing a dinner jacket! Maybe it's going to a party!"

"If there's a party, I wouldn't know about it, Pooh."

Just Hatched!

A baby penguin is called a chick. It took two months for this fuzzy chick to hatch. Can you see how its daddy keeps it warm?

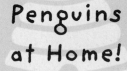

Growing Up!

What's for dinner? Fresh fish from the ocean! The chick's mummy and daddy take turns feeding it.

Penguins at Home!

Br-r-r! Some penguins live in Antarctica. They waddle on the ice. They slide on the snow. They dive deep into the cold water.

Hello, Ostrich!

"Piglet, that ostrich is running so fast, I need to sit down and rest!"

Just Hatched!

What big eggs! Each one is 20 times bigger than a chicken egg. All the mummy ostriches lay their eggs in one big nest.

Growing Up!

One by one, off the baby ostriches go.
They follow their mummy.
They are only a few weeks old.
But they were born ready to run.

Ostriches at Home!

Many ostriches live in Africa. Unlike most birds, they do not live in trees. Why not? Ostriches cannot fly! They are too heavy. An ostrich is 90,000 times heavier than a hummingbird!

Roo
Wants to Know...

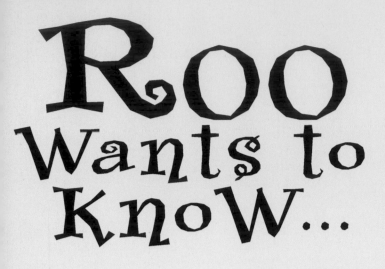

Can penguins fly?

Penguins cannot fly in the sky. But they certainly can swim. Penguins are fast and graceful under the water.

Do ducks get cold in the water?

No. Ducks have special feathers to protect them. This keeps the water from getting to their skin underneath. Ducks also have soft, fluffy down feathers to keep them warm.

Why do owls turn their heads so far around?

Owls cannot move their eyes from side to side the way people do. So, to see all around them, they turn their heads instead.

Why is a peacock's tail so big and colourful?

It is only the male peacock that has such a fancy tail. Male peacocks use their tails to show off. A male will fan out his tail to show a female how beautiful he is.

Do parrots talk?

Yes. They listen to the sounds around them. They repeat what they hear. Since many people have parrots as pets, some can bark like a dog, meow like a cat, and even say the alphabet!

Why are flamingos pink?

Flamingos are pink because of the food they eat. The teeny, tiny shrimp they scoop up in the water make their feathers turn pink!

Hello, Parrot!

"Parrots, Pooh, are very clever birds. I'd like to have a chat with that fellow!"
"I'll wait for you here, Owl!"

Just Hatched!

These baby parrots have just hatched. Where are their feathers? Like many birds, parrots are born without them.

Growing Up!

Look at their feathers now! The parrots have grown a lot in just one month. They clean and groom each other.

Parrots at Home!

"*Squawk, squawk!*" Noisy parrots call to one another in the tropical forests. Parrots like to be with their friends. Sometimes 80 or more live together.

Hello, Peacock!

"Now that's what I call a tail, Pooh!"

These brown baby peafowl are called peachicks. It takes two years for peacocks to get their beautiful tail feathers. But just a few hours after hatching, they walk around, showing off their little brown tails.

Growing Up!

When peachicks are hungry, they peck at their mummy's beak. She feeds them. Soon they will peck at the ground and feed themselves. See how different they look from the time when they were hatched.

Peacocks at Home!

Peacocks live in India. They live in nests on the ground. They also like to rest on tree branches. It is safer for them to be up high.

83

Hello, Eagle!

"That eagle is a beautiful, big bird, Owl!"
"Yes, indeed, Pooh. But not as beautiful
as an owl, of course."

Just Hatched!

Baby eagles are called eaglets. These fuzzy eaglets were inside their eggs for about a month. Their mummy and daddy took turns sitting on the eggs until they hatched.

Growing Up!

Look who is hungry! These baby eagles are fed by both their mummy and daddy. They need their parents until they learn to fly. That will be in just a few months.

Eagles at Home!

Eagles live high up in trees or on cliffs. They often build nests near lakes and rivers. That is so they can dive down and fish for their food.

84

THAT'S TIGGERIFIC!

Arctic terns fly all around the world once a year.

They fly from the North Pole to the South Pole, and then back again. That is a total of 18,000 miles.

A woodpecker can bang away at a tree and not hurt its head.

That is because woodpeckers have extra-strong bones in their heads. It is as if they have their own built-in helmets!

Ostriches are the biggest birds in the world.

They can be nine feet tall and weigh more than 300 pounds.

Eagles build huge nests.

The nests can be as big as two of you! That is because the eagles keep adding on to the same nest year after year.

Peregrine falcons are the fastest birds in the world.

They can dive down from the skies at 112 mph (180 kph). That is almost twice as fast as a car speeding down the motorway!

Hoo, hoo, hoo!

Puffins are the only birds that shed their beaks. All other birds have beaks that grow with them. But puffins lose scales from their beak as they grow.

Look and Find with Piglet!

Now you've learnt about birds, look at the picture and answer the questions below.

- How many birds are in this picture?
- What bird is swimming in the pond?
- How many birds are flying?
- Can you find the bird's nest?
- How many eggs are in the bird's nest?
- How many birds are completely blue?
- How many completely yellow birds are there?
- Can you find the woodpecker?

Answers

- 14
- A duck
- 4
- It's in the grass
- 4
- 5
- 2
- It is on the fence

Chapter 3

REPTILES & AMPHIBIANS

Pooh Wonders . . .

One day, on the way to his Thoughtful Spot, Pooh saw Eeyore standing by the river.

"Hello, Eeyore," Pooh said. "What are you doing?"

"I'm just passing the time by watching that rock, Pooh," Eeyore replied.

"Er, why are you doing that, Eeyore?" Pooh asked.

"Nothing better to do," Eeyore said sadly. "Besides, I saw it move. I want to see if it does it again."

Pooh scratched his head. "I don't think rocks are supposed to move, Eeyore."

"I tried to tell it that," Eeyore sighed. "That's when it stopped moving."

Pooh stared at the rock. Only it didn't look quite so much like a rock any more – not unless rocks usually have legs and a head.

"Eeyore," Pooh cried. "I don't think it's a rock at all. In fact, I'm quite sure that it's a turtle!"

"Oh I see."

Pooh waited for his friend to say something else. But Eeyore just sat there silently.

"What are you doing now, Eeyore?" Pooh asked.

Eeyore shrugged. "Just passing the time by watching that turtle, Pooh."

"Come on, let's meet some reptiles and amphibians!"

91

A turtle is a reptile with a hard shell.

A gecko is a reptile that hatches from an egg that's about the size of a peanut.

"Owl, what is a reptile?"

A reptile is an animal.

Many reptiles have curly tails, long snouts, or hard shells.

Some reptiles can even change colour!

Some reptiles have smooth skin, and some have bumpy skin.

An iguana is a reptile that likes to climb.

A crocodile is a big reptile with a long snout.

A snake is a long skinny reptile with no legs.

"So, what makes an animal a reptile?"

- All reptiles are cold blooded. This means their bodies have the same temperature as their surroundings.
- All reptiles have dry skin.
- All reptiles are covered with scales. Scales are hard, dry pieces of skin that protect a reptile's body.

A chameleon is a reptile with horns on its nose.

Hello, Turtle!

"That looks like an awfully messy place to eat dinner!"

Just Hatched!

Look! This baby turtle has hatched from its egg. Before it hatched, its mummy dug a nest hole. She laid her eggs in the hole and covered them with dirt. The dirt keeps the eggs warm.

Growing Up!

As soon as this turtle hatched, it headed straight to the water for its very first swim! This turtle is growing up. Now it mostly eats insects. When it gets bigger, it will munch on plants, too.

Turtles at Home!

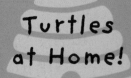

Many turtles live in the water. Different kinds of turtles can be found in streams, ponds, and in the sea. Other kinds of turtles live on land. You can even find turtles out in the desert!

Hello, Crocodile!

"Piglet, perhaps now is not the very best time for a swim. I think I'll take a nap instead!"

Just Hatched!

Here it comes! This little crocodile is poking its way out of its egg. Like all reptiles, it has a special tooth called an egg tooth. It uses its egg tooth to cut through the tough eggshell.

Growing Up!

"Squeak! Squeak!" This baby crocodile makes that sound so its mummy can find it. Then it takes a ride in a very safe place!

Crocodiles at Home!

Ahhh! That feels good! This crocodile is cooling off in the water. Crocodiles live in rivers and lakes in very warm places. They like to bake on the sand or in the mud near the edges of the water.

Hello, Snake!

"Owl, why would these fellows stick their tongues out at us? What did we do?"
"They're not being rude, Pooh. They're actually sniffing the air!"

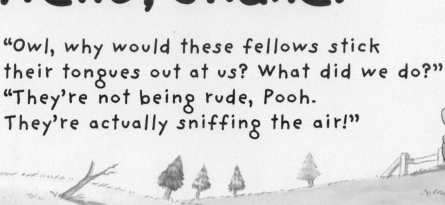

Just Hatched!

These tiny garter snakes have just been born. Unlike most snakes, garter snakes do not hatch from eggs. Baby garter snakes can take care of themselves as soon as they are born.

Growing Up!

This young garter snake is growing very quickly. It will be fully grown one year after it is born. It may grow to be about four feet long.

Snakes at Home!

Snakes can be found all over the world. They live in rainforests, woodlands, swamps, and deserts. Most snakes live in warm places.

Hello, Iguana!

"That iguana is a lovely shade of green, Pooh!"
"Yes, indeed, Piglet!"

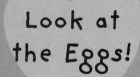

Look at the Eggs!

Mummy iguanas can lay up to 70 eggs at a time! They lay their eggs in sandy areas. It is easy for the babies to dig out of the nest when they hatch.

Growing Up!

A young iguana looks just like its mummy. It could grow to be about six feet long! Do you think you'll grow that tall?

Iguanas at Home!

There are many different kinds of iguanas. They can be found in deserts and rainforests, and on islands. Iguanas live in many places around the world. One kind of iguana even lives in the ocean!

THAT'S TIGGERIFIC!

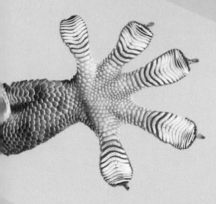

Geckos can walk upside down.

They have special bristles on their feet that help them hold on to things. That's why they can hang upside down without falling!

Did you know that a crocodile has 60 to 80 teeth in its mouth?

That's more than twice as many as you have! Whenever it loses a tooth, a crocodile grows a new one in the old tooth's place!

Some frogs sleep through the long, cold winter.

They snuggle down into muddy beds and fall fast asleep! Then, they wake up and hop around again when it gets warm.

What happens if a lizard is chased and grabbed by its tail?

Not to worry. Some lizards can break away from their tails. And after a while, they will grow a new one.

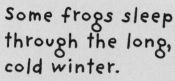

Sea snakes can swim without getting water up their nose.

They close off their nostrils while they are under the water.

When a turtle feels afraid, it hides inside its shell.

That's right! It just tucks its head, legs, and tail totally inside. It's like it's shutting the door to its house!

Hello, Gecko!

"Now, that gecko is right side up, Piglet!"
"But Pooh, now we're upside down!"

Look at the Eggs!

Look at the tiny gecko eggs! Each one is about the size of a peanut! Mummy geckos usually lay two eggs at a time. The eggs have very hard shells that protect the babies inside until they are ready to hatch.

Hatching and Growing!

This little gecko is hatching from its egg! It grew inside its egg for six months. Now it looks just like its mummy.

Geckos at Home!

Geckos live in warm areas all over the world. Some geckos live in rainforests. Others live in dry deserts. Still others live in the mountains!

Hello, Chameleon!

"I can't seem to turn any colour other than plain old grey, can I, Pooh?"

Look at the Eggs!

Look who's on the way! Baby chameleons are soon going to hatch from their eggs! Their eggs are about the width of a 20p coin.

Growing Up!

Up, up, up! Baby chameleons head for the safety of trees as soon as they hatch. They already know how to find food and water. When a chameleon grows up, it will be about as long as your arm is now.

Chameleons at Home!

Chameleons are happiest in very warm places. Many chameleons live in the forests of India and Africa. They are all great climbers! Their special claws help them to hold on to tree branches.

Hello, Goanna!

"Is that goanna looking at us, Pooh?"
"I don't know about that, Piglet. I do know we're looking at it!"

Look at the Eggs!

Look what's here! It's a newborn goanna. Baby goannas are called hatchlings. This goanna is just hatching out of its shell. Its mummy laid 11 eggs in all.

Hatching and Growing

As a young goanna grows, it learns many things. This one has learned how to look scary. Standing up on its back legs is one way it protects itself.

Goannas at Home!

Some goannas are also called sand monitor lizards. That is because they live on dry, sandy soil. They need to sit in the sun to stay warm. And there is nothing like a nice, warm rock to do that.

Roo Wants to Know...

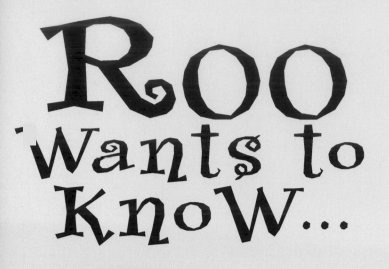

Do turtles have teeth?

No. A turtle cuts its food using its sharp beak. It is a lot like a bird's beak. Then the turtle mashes up the food with its strong jaws.

Do snakes have ears?

No. They hear by feeling. How do they do that? When something moves, snakes can feel the vibrations in the ground.

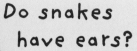

Can snakes swim?

Yes. Many snakes can swim.
The biggest snake in the world,
the anaconda, spends most of
its time in the water.

Can you get warts from touching a toad?

No. Even though toads have bumps
on their skin, they are not warts. So,
toads don't have warts, and they
don't give warts.

Why does a frilled lizard have a "collar"?

That is extra skin.
The lizard puffs
it up when it is
afraid. This makes
it look bigger. And it
hopes it will make it
look scary
to its enemies.

How can you tell the difference between a crocodile and an alligator?

They are very alike. But look here: crocodiles have long, thin
pointy snouts; alligators have wide snouts. When a crocodile
closes its mouth, you can see the teeth from the lower jaw
pointing upwards. When an alligator closes its mouth,
you can see its top teeth pointing downward.

A toad is an amphibian with bumpy skin.

A triton is an amphibian, too!

"Owl, what is an amphibian?"

An amphibian is an animal, too! Many amphibians have long tails. Some amphibians can leap high in the air. Other amphibians even have webbed feet.

Baby amphibians usually hatch in the water. A baby amphibian is called a larva. Baby frogs and toads are called tadpoles. Both larvae and tadpoles look very different from their parents.

A salamander is an amphibian that has different colours.

A salamander is an amphibian that hides under leaves.

"So, what makes an animal an amphibian?"

- Most amphibians live in or around water.
- All amphibians keep their skin a little wet.
- All amphibians are cold blooded, just like reptiles.
- Amphibian eggs look like beads of jelly and don't have hard shells.

A frog is an amphibian with webbed feet.

This frog is an amphibian that lives in flowers.

Hello, Frog!

"Ribbit! Ribbit!"

Just Hatched!

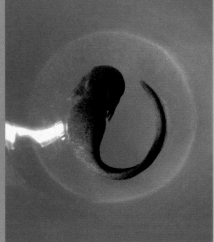

It's time for newborn frogs! A baby frog is called a tadpole. A tadpole has a large head, a round body, and a long tail. It uses its long tail to help it swim as soon as it is born.

Growing Up!

Look! This tadpole is growing up. First, its body gets fatter. It starts to grow legs and will lose its tail. Then it will be a froglet.

Frogs at Home!

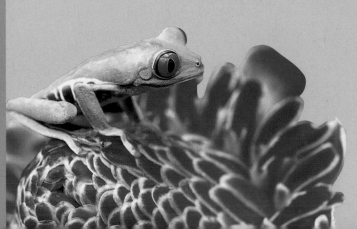

Frogs can be found all over the world. They usually live in wet areas near ponds, lakes, and rivers. Some frogs even live in trees.

Hello, Toad!

"My, what big eyes it has, Pooh!"
"All the better to see you with, Piglet!"

Look at the Eggs!

This mother toad is laying her eggs in the water. The eggs look like little strings of beads. Some mummy toads can lay up to 12,000 eggs at one time!

Growing Up!

A toad starts out as a tadpole, just like a frog does. Once it has grown its legs and lost its tail, the toad tadpole will become a toadlet.

Toads at Home!

Toads can be found on leafy forest floors, in wet swamps, and even in deserts. One place you will not find toads is in the ocean. They cannot live in the salty water!

Hello, Salamander!

"Look, Pooh! That salamander looks like it's fallen into some paint!"

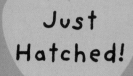
Just Hatched!

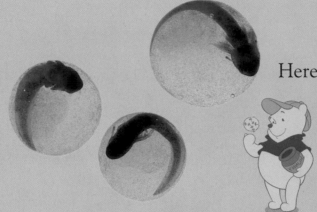

Here come the baby salamanders! Before they hatched, the babies grew inside their eggs for two or three weeks.

Growing Up!

Most salamanders grow up in the water. Their legs grow longer so that they'll be ready to crawl on land. Some salamanders grow up in five or six weeks. Others can take up to five years!

Salamanders at Home!

Most salamanders live in cool, dark places. You might find a salamander hiding under a log or a rock. Salamanders usually live close to the water, because that's where a mummy salamander lays her eggs.

THAT'S TIGGERIFIC!

The Japanese giant salamander can grow to be five feet long.

It would take up the whole back seat of a car! How would you like to have one on your next car trip?

This mummy crocodile is not eating her babies.

She is being a very protective parent. This is how mummy crocodiles carry their newly hatched babies to a safe place.

As snakes grow, their skin gets too small for their bodies.

They wriggle around until the old skin comes off. Underneath, they have fresh new skin that's just the right size!

Hoo, hoo, hoo!

When a goanna is in danger, it stands up on its hind legs. Then it runs away, just using its back legs.

Chameleons use their tails like extra hands.

They wrap their curly tails around tree branches to hang on. Now that's Tiggerific!

Look and Find with Piglet!

Now you've learned about reptiles and amphibians, look at the picture and answer the questions below.

- How many reptiles can you find?

- What is Tigger playing with?

- How many amphibians are there?

- How many turtles can you find?

- How many frogs are jumping?

- Can you find the salamander?

- What is the frog sitting on?

- What has its house on its back?

Chapter 4

SEA CREATURES

Pooh Wonders . . .

Pooh was sitting in his Thoughtful Spot when raindrops started to fall.

"Oh bother," Pooh said. "I suppose that's enough thinking for today."

He hurried through the rain towards the closest shelter, which happened to be Kanga and Roo's house.

"What are you doing, Roo?" Pooh asked.

"Jumping up and down in a puddle. I'm pretending to be a fish, Pooh Bear!" Roo said.

"A fish?" Pooh asked. "Is that a kind of Roo that jumps in the rain?"

Roo laughed. "No, Pooh. A fish is a kind of creature that lives underwater."

Pooh looked up. "Well, I suppose we are underwater," he said, "since water is falling from over us right now."

"That's not what I mean, Pooh," Roo said. "Mama says lots of different creatures live underwater. Come inside, and maybe she'll tell us more about them."

"That sounds like a nice, dry sort of idea." Pooh agreed, following Roo towards the door. "I don't suppose there's any honey underwater?"

"I don't think so, Pooh," Roo replied. "But don't worry. There's plenty inside our house."

"Come on, let's meet some sea creatures!"

125

A sea anemone is a sea creature, too!

A dolphin can jump high out of the water.

A clown fish is a brightly coloured fish

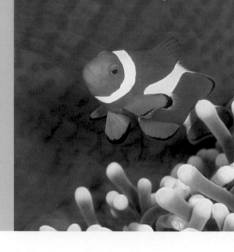

"Owl, what is a sea creature?"

A sea creature is an animal that lives in or around the sea.

All of the animals on these pages are sea creatures.

Some sea creatures are mammals. Sea mammals cannot stay underwater all the time. They have to come up to the surface to breathe the air.

Other sea creatures have shells, long arms, or sharp claws, and stay underwater most of the time.

A hermit crab is a sea creature that has its own house.

A shark
is a fish with
a long nose.

"So, what makes a
sea creature a fish?"

- All fish have fins.
- All fish have gills to help them breathe
  underwater all the time.

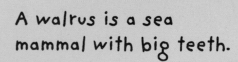

A walrus is a sea
mammal with big teeth.

A starfish is a
sea creature with
five arms

Hello, Clown Fish!

"Pooh, I thought all clowns had big red noses and wore floppy shoes."

Just Hatched!

Look! These baby clown fish are hatching from their eggs. A mummy clown fish lays almost 200 eggs at one time. That makes for a lot of babies! Newborn clown fish are so tiny that you could hold all 200 of them in your hand! When they are this young, clown fish don't look like their mummies and daddies yet.

Growing Up!

Up, up, up! Baby clown fish swim to the top of the water as soon as they hatch. They are looking for food. Once the clown fish have each grown to about the size of a raisin, they swim back down. Then they look for homes.

Clown Fish at Home!

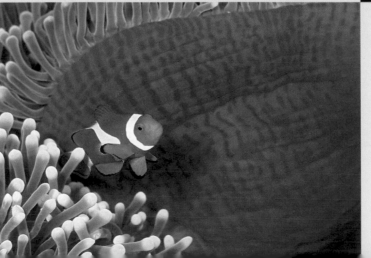

Clown fish live underwater in coral reefs. They stay near animals called sea anemones. Sea anemones are dangerous to other fish, but not to clown fish. This is how clown fish stay safe.

128

Hello, Dolphin!

"Look, Piglet. That dolphin is smiling at us. Let's smile back!"

Just Born!

Look at the baby dolphin being born! A newborn dolphin is called a calf. As soon as a baby dolphin is born, it swims up for a breath of air. Then it returns for a drink of its mummy's milk. Dolphins are sea mammals.

Growing Up!

These calves and their mummies live in family groups called schools. A baby dolphin will stay with its mummy for three to six years. Then it will join a school of other young dolphins.

Dolphins at Home!

Dolphins live in oceans all over the world. They are often friendly and playful. If you go to the beach, you might see dolphins jumping out of the water!

Hello, Shark!

"Do not fear that whale shark, Piglet. It may be the biggest fish in the world, but it is a very peaceful animal."

Just Born!

Baby sharks are called pups. A mummy shark will look for a safe place to have her babies. But mummy and daddy sharks don't take care of their babies after they are born.

Growing Up!

There are many different kinds of sharks. Some will be fully grown when they are as small as a pencil. Other sharks will grow to weigh as much as two elephants!

Sharks at Home!

Sharks live in ocean waters all over the world. Some sharks live in rivers and lakes, too. Unlike other fish that can swim backwards and forwards, sharks can only swim forwards.

Hello, Hermit Crab!

"Let's be sure to stay out of its way, Piglet!"
"I'm with you, Pooh. Those claws look awfully strong!"

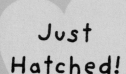

Just Hatched!

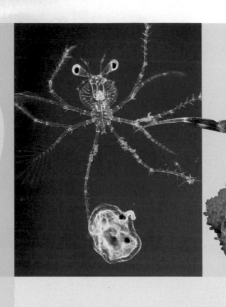

This baby hermit crab has just hatched! Before it hatched, its mummy carried her eggs in a special place under her body.

Growing Up!

A young hermit crab has a very soft body. It needs to find a hard shell to slip into to keep it safe. Empty snail shells are a perfect fit! As a hermit crab grows, it will need to find bigger snail shells to wear. That's just like you getting new clothes each time you grow!

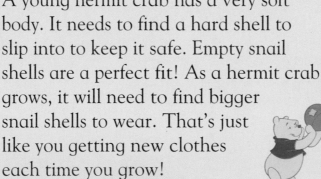

Hermit Crabs at Home!

Hermit crabs live on land or in the water. A hermit crab walks along on its eight legs, looking for plants and animals to eat. It grabs things with its two big claws.

THAT'S TIGGERIFIC!

Large groups of spiny lobsters travel every year for warmer weather.

Each one links its claws to the lobster in front of it. Then they all move along in single file beneath the sea. Sometimes there are as many as 50 lobsters hooked up together! Now that's Tiggerific!

A Tigger only needs two feet. But a starfish uses many more to crawl around.

Under their arms, called rays, they have little feet called tube feet. Each starfish has hundreds of these tube feet.

Did you know that mummy and daddy sea horses meet every morning?

To greet one another, they turn a brighter colour. Then they might go for a swim with their tails hooked together.

Hermit crabs have tiny little hairs that help them feel things that they touch.

This is how they know what is around them in the water.

A sea otter is an animal that loves the sea.

These mammals have very thick fur. It is so thick that their skin, underneath, never gets wet.

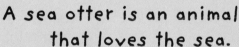

You might think that a snail crawls on its belly.

But the bottom part of a snail is really its foot.

Hello, Sea Horse!

"Piglet, I wonder who could be small enough to ride on that horse?!"

Just Born!

Look! These baby sea horses have just hatched. The daddy sea horse carried the eggs inside his pouch. The daddy sea horse is the only male sea creature who takes care of his babies' eggs before they are born. That makes him a pretty special daddy!

Growing Up!

Sea horses can take care of themselves as soon as they are born. They have to help one another swim, though, because their tiny fins are not very strong. They hold onto one another's tails. Just like friends!

Sea Horses at Home!

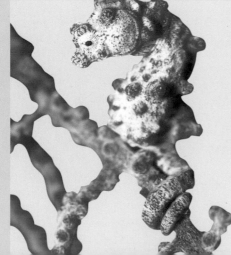

Sea horses live in warm waters. Many sea horses live in coral reefs. Sea horses are good at hiding. They blend in with the colours of the coral reef.

Hello, Octopus!

"If I had to swim with that many legs, Pooh, I'd just get all tangled up!"

Just Hatched!

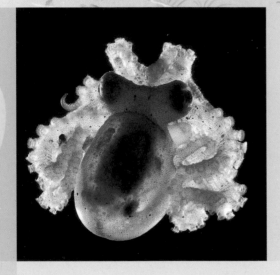

This baby octopus has hatched from its egg. A mummy octopus lays thousands of eggs at a time. The babies are small enough to sit on your little finger!

Growing Up!

After hatching, the baby octopuses float around near the top of the water. They don't know how to crawl or swim yet. A few weeks later, they float back down to the seabed. Then they start to grow up.

Octopuses at Home!

Octopuses live in underwater dens. They can crawl into some very small spaces! When an octopus gets hungry, it moves through the water and looks for crabs to eat.

Hello, Starfish!

"Pooh, do you think that fellow is important?"
"Piglet, I do believe it's the star of the ocean!"

This baby starfish has hatched its egg. Baby starfish will float around the sea for two months after they hatch. They will do a lot of growing while they are floating.
Starfish are also known as sea stars. They are not actually fish.

Look at this starfish growing up. Can you see little starfish arms beginning to grow? Starfish arms are called rays. Sometimes a starfish might lose a ray. If it does, it will grow a new one!

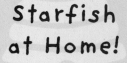

Most starfish live on the ocean floor. Some starfish live near the shore in little pools of water called rock pools. You might even see a starfish when you are at the beach!

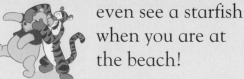

Hello, Manatee!

"Pooh, that fellow looks awfully sad. I know just how it feels!"

Just Born!

Look at this newborn manatee calf. It weighs about 65 pounds. That's almost 10 times as much as you weighed when you were born! A manatee is a mammal. The baby has to swim up to get air as soon as it is born. It's good it is born knowing how to swim!

Growing Up!

The baby manatee is growing. It will stay with its mummy until it is two years old. The calf will drink its mummy's milk and look for plants to eat. This manatee calf is getting a ride from its mummy!

Manatees at Home!

Yum! This manatee has found some plants to munch on. Manatees live in river systems and use the ocean to get from one place to another.

Roo Wants to Know...

How does an octopus eat?

An octopus uses its arms to put food in its mouth. Its arms have suckers that are sticky, and they hold on to the food.

How do whales breathe?

Since a whale is a mammal, it breathes through its lungs and must come up for air. It will stick its head out of the water and breathe through a special hole in its head. It is called a blowhole. Whales breathe through this blowhole the way people breathe through their nose.

How does a jellyfish swim?

A jellyfish pushes itself through the water. Its body looks like an umbrella. It is called a bell. The jellyfish opens and closes the bell, and this helps it move.

Do dolphins talk to one another?

Yes. They whistle, chirp, squeak, and click to one another under the water. They also talk to one another without sound. They will move about, and do something that looks like a little dance.

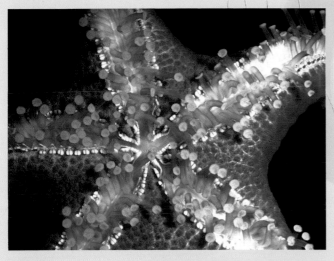

Where is a starfish's mouth?

A starfish's mouth is on its belly. To eat, it crawls over its food.

What does a walrus use its long teeth for?

A walrus's long teeth are called tusks. The tusks are good for digging into the hard ice. This helps the walrus climb onto icy rocks. Walruses also dig in the sandy ocean floor to look for shellfish.

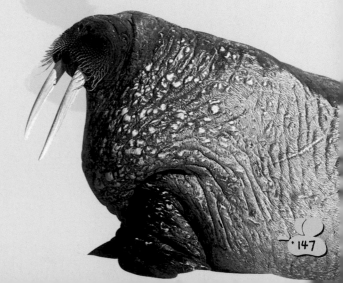

147

Hello, Walrus!

"Piglet, it must take that walrus a long time to brush its teeth!"

Just Born!

Look! This walrus calf is being nursed by its mummy. It weighed more than 100 pounds when it was born. That's as much as 10 bowling balls put together! How much did you weigh when you were born?

Growing Up!

At only one month old, this baby walrus is already a very good swimmer. A baby walrus and its mummy live with other walrus mummies and babies. As a baby walrus grows, its coat changes from grey to a rusty-brown colour.

Walruses at Home!

Brrrr! Walruses live in icy, cold oceans. They huddle together to keep warm. Walruses have fatty blubber on their bodies that also helps keep them warm.

148

Hello, Sea Anemone!

"Piglet, why are you wearing that silly hat?"
"So I can be as beautiful as that sea creature!"

Just Hatched!

This baby sea anemone has just hatched! These sea creatures don't look at all like their mummies and daddies when they hatch.
Baby sea anemones are called planulae.

Growing Up!

The tiny baby sea anemones float around in the water. They have little hairs that help them move through the water. After a while, the young sea anemones come back down to the ocean floor. They find a place in which to live, and they start to grow. Soon they will have arms and tentacles like grown-up sea anemones.

Sea Anemones at Home!

Many sea anemones live on rocks or on coral. Sea anemones don't move around a lot. They like to stay in one place. They can move if they need to by walking on their tentacles.

Hello, Jellyfish!

"Pooh, doesn't that animal look like a balloon?"
"Yes, it does Piglet"

Just Born!

Look at all the tiny baby jellyfish! They've just hatched from their eggs. Baby jellyfish are born without arms or tentacles. They float in the water until they find a rock or a shell to sit on. Then they will start growing!

Growing Up!

Look at this jellyfish growing up! If you look closely, you can even see its little tentacles growing.

Jellyfish at Home!

Jellyfish live in oceans all around the world. There are many kinds of jellyfish. Some are so small, you can't see them. Others grow to be bigger than grown-up people!

Not all sharks are plain looking.

Some have polka dots. Whale sharks have bright white spots and stripes all over their bodies. And isn't that Tiggerific?

An octopus is a very colourful creature.

It will change its colour when it is afraid, angry, or happy. It will also change its colour when it is hiding.

Manatees can hold their breath underwater for a long time.

They can stay under for about 15 minutes before they need to come up for air.

THAT'S TIGGERIFIC!

These fish don't really fly, but they look like they can.

Flying fish come out of the water as fast as 20 mph. They can glide over the water as far as 1,300 feet.

Boxer crabs carry sea anemones around with them.

They "wear" them on their claws like mittens. Then they wave them around to scare off any hungry fish that might come near them.

Look here!

This type of fish has its own little lights. Lantern fish light up under the water. They have a special way of making their bodies glow.

Look and Find with Piglet!

Now you've learned about sea creatures, look at the picture and answer the questions below.

- How many paintings of sea creatures are there?
- Find the sea horse.
- How many fish can you see?
- What is Tigger painting?
- Which sea creature has tusks?
- Find the painting of the dolphin.
- Which sea creature has lots of teeth?
- How many paintings are hanging in the trees?

- The fish and the sea horse.
- The shark
- It's on the bridge.
- The walrus
- A starfish
- 7
- It is hanging from the tree's branch.
- 6

Answers

Chapter 5

INSECTS
& SPIDERS

Pooh Wonders . . .

One day, when Piglet was feeling especially small, Pooh was trying to make him feel better.

"Don't be sad, Piglet," Pooh said. "Even small creatures can do big things."

Pooh led Piglet outside to Rabbit's garden. "Just look closely," Pooh said.

Soon, Piglet saw a tiny ant. The ant was carrying a fallen leaf much bigger than itself.

"Oh my!" Pooh said. "That's quite a large leaf for a little creature to carry."

Next Pooh noticed a dragonfly flitting around the clearing.

"Oh my!" he said. "You move quite fast for such a little fellow."

The dragonfly zipped away.

As Pooh watched it go, he noticed a spider building a web nearby.

"Oh my!" he said. "That's quite a fancy web for such a little spider to weave."

Pooh said to Piglet, "See! Being small isn't so bad."

"I guess anybody can do really big things – even me!" Piglet said, smiling.

"Come on, let's meet some insects and spiders!"

Butterflies are insects that live all around the world.

A dragonfly is an insect that lives near water.

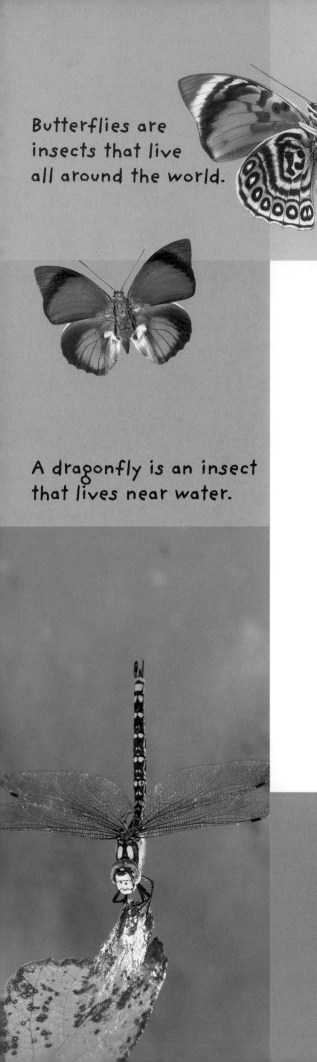

"Owl, what is an insect?"

An insect is an animal.

Insects are everywhere!

There are more insects in the world than there are any other animal.

Insects have been on the earth for a very long time. They were here even before the dinosaurs!

Insects come in all different shapes, sizes, and colours.

A ladybird is an insect that protects flowers.

An ant is an insect that has a very big family.

"So, what makes an animal an insect?"

- Every insect has three parts to its body.
- Every insect has six legs.
- Every insect has its skeleton on the outside of its body!

A grasshopper is an insect that likes to jump.

A bee is an insect that makes honey.

Hello, Bee!

"*I am all rumbly in my tumbly, watching that bee. You don't suppose it's going to go make some honey, do you, Piglet?*"

Hatching and Growing!

Baby honeybees grow inside a honeycomb. They begin as tiny eggs. Once they hatch, they will eat the yummy honey.

Creeping, Crawling, and Flying

"Buzz, buzz." Bees fly from flower to flower. They sip the sweet nectar. Then they fly off to look for more! They collect pollen on their legs as they go from flower to flower.

Bees at Home!

Bees like to be with other bees. They live in very large groups. There might be 60,000 bees in just one hive!

Hello, Ladybird!

"Look, Eeyore! That insect is dressed in polka dots!"
"Polka dots make me look fat!"

Hatching and Growing!

This mummy ladybird found a safe place to lay her eggs. Her babies will hatch after four days. At first, they will look like tiny worms called larvae.

Creeping, Crawling, and Flying

Like most other insects, the ladybird has wings. But they are hidden! There are hard wing cases on top of a ladybird's real wings. Can you see this ladybird's wings?

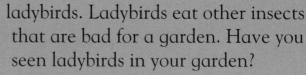

Ladybirds at Home!

Ladybirds live around plants. People like ladybirds. Ladybirds eat other insects that are bad for a garden. Have you seen ladybirds in your garden?

Hello, Ant!

"Look, Pooh. That ant can carry something as big as itself!"

Hatching and Growing!

Like all insects, these ants hatched from eggs. They are called antlings. Sisters in a nest help take care of the new babies.

Creeping, Crawling, and Flying

Look! This ant is strong. It is bringing food back to its nest.

Ants at Home!

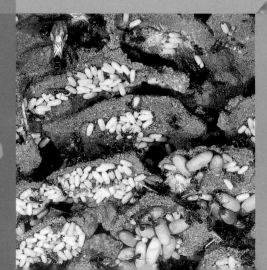

Ants live together in a big group called a colony. Ants are very good builders. They make long tunnels underground.

Hello, Grasshopper!

"That grasshopper does some very nice jumping, Pooh!"

Hatching and Growing!

This baby grasshopper is called a nymph. It looks just like a grown-up grasshopper. But it is tiny and has no wings yet.

Creeping, Crawling, and Flying

A grasshopper can fly. It can walk. And it can hop. That is a lot of different ways in which to move! In what way do you like to move?

Grasshoppers at Home!

Grasshoppers live in meadows, fields, and even gardens. They live where they can find tasty plants to eat.

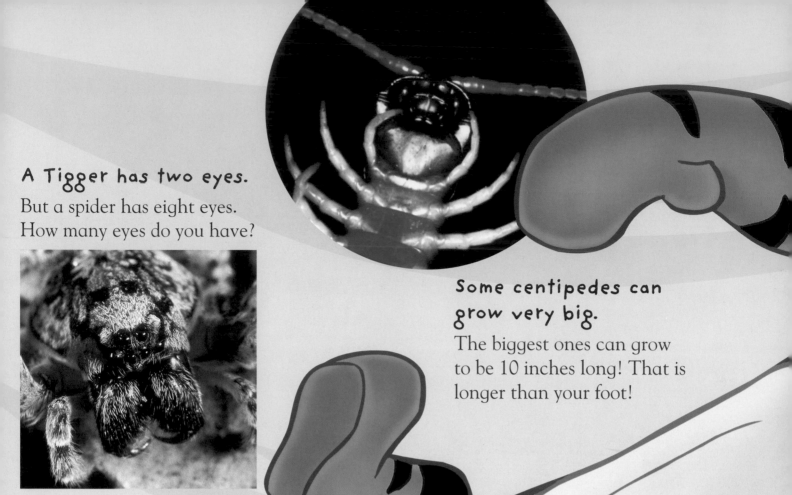

A Tigger has two eyes.
But a spider has eight eyes.
How many eyes do you have?

Some centipedes can
grow very big.
The biggest ones can grow
to be 10 inches long! That is
longer than your foot!

Some insects look just like
green leaves.
That helps them hide and stay
safe. Can you see the insect in
this picture?

THAT'S TIGGERIFIC!

People aren't the only ones who can make paper.

Wasps make their nests out of paper. They chew on wood, then turn it into paper.

The largest butterflies look like small birds when they fly.

They are called Queen Alexandra's bird wing butterflies. Their wings are more than 10 inches across.

Tiggers like to bounce.

And grasshoppers like to jump. Grasshoppers can jump further than any other insect. They can jump 20 times their own length!

Hello, Cricket!

"That is very nice of you, Piglet, to help the cricket sing its tune."
"Thank you, Pooh!"

Hatching and Growing!

Could you sing when you were born? Baby crickets – as tiny as grains of rice and also called nymphs – are born knowing how to sing their special cricket song.

Creeping, Crawling, and Flying

Crickets use their wings to fly. Male crickets also use their wings to sing to females. A cricket rubs its wings together to make a chirping sound.

Crickets at Home!

Have you ever heard a cricket sing at night? Night is the time when crickets like to be out and about. During the day, they sleep under rocks and logs.

Hello, Butterfly!

"That butterfly is really enjoying the flower, Pooh."
"Yes, Piglet. It makes me want a smackerel of honey!"

Hatching and Growing!

How does a butterfly grow? A butterfly begins as a caterpillar. It eats, eats, eats all day. Then it becomes a pupa. The caterpillar stays inside the pupa as it grows into a butterfly. Welcome, butterfly!

Creeping, Crawling, and Flying

Butterflies have very beautiful wings. They come in all different colours. What colours do you see on these butterflies?

Butterflies at Home!

Butterflies live among flowers. They sip the nectar with their long tongues. Some butterflies travel hundreds of miles to find warm weather.

Hello, Centipede!

"Look at all those legs and feet on that centipede, Piglet!"
"Oh, Pooh, I hope it's not ticklish!"

Hatching and Growing!

Centipedes are creepy crawlies that are close relatives of insects. Mummy centipedes lay about 60 eggs at a time. First they dig a hole; then they safely drop the eggs in.

Creeping, Crawling, and Flying

Look at all those legs! Some centipedes have 140 legs! That is why they can move very fast.

Centipedes at Home!

Centipedes like wet, damp places. They also like the dark. They squeeze themselves under logs and rocks and enjoy themselves!

Hello, Dragonfly!

"My, that dragonfly can fly fast, Eeyore!"
"Too fast for me, Pooh!"

Hatching and Growing!

This baby dragonfly was hatched underwater. It is called a nymph. It has no wings yet. The nymph is growing!

The dragonfly is now all grown up. It has its wings. It is ready to fly.

Creeping, Crawling, and Flying

Dragonflies love to fly. They even eat while they are flying. They catch insects in their mouth while they are in midair!

Dragonflies at Home!

Dragonflies live all around water. You can see them fly – and hear them buzz! – near ponds and lakes.

Roo
Wants to Know...

Do all bees make honey?
No. There are many kinds of bees. Honeybees are the ones that make honey.

How can you tell the difference between a moth and a butterfly?
One way to tell is to look at them while they are resting. Butterflies rest with their wings folded up. A moth will rest with its wings spread out. Is this a picture of a moth or a butterfly?

Do all spiders spin webs?
Not all of them. Some spiders catch their food by making other kinds of traps. This spider has dug a tunnel, using its fangs. It sits and waits for its dinner to "drop by."

How do ants find their way without getting lost?

Ants find their way by using their sense of smell. Once their noses pick up a smell, they follow it. They just keep on following the smell until it leads them back home.

Do ants talk to each other?

Yes. Ants use their feelers to talk to each other. Feelers are long hairs that come out of an ant's head. When two ants touch their feelers, they are telling each other where the food is.

Are all ladybirds red?

No. Ladybirds come in all different colours. Some are yellow; others are orange. Even the red ones are different shades of red.

Some spiders are
hard to see.

Some spiders are furry.

"Owl, what is a spider?"

A spider is an animal.

Spiders crawl, climb, and walk all around us.

There are almost 40,000 different kinds of spiders!

Spiders can be as tiny as the head of a pin, or they can be bigger than your hand.

Some spiders live
in trees.

Some spiders look scary.

"So, what makes a spider a spider?"

- Spiders have eight legs.
- A spider has only two parts to its body.
- Most spiders make webs. They build them from silk. The silk comes from a spider's tummy.

This spider spins a very nice web.

Hello, Spider!

"How does a spider make such a pretty web, Pooh?"
"Maybe it can teach us, Piglet!"

Hatching and Growing!

Look at all these baby spiders! They are called spiderlings. They hatched from eggs.
Their mummy kept the eggs safe by wrapping them in her silk.

Creeping, Crawling, and Flying

Have you ever wondered why a spider can crawl all over its web and not get stuck?

Its tiny feet have a special oil on them. The oil makes the web slippery so they don't get stuck!

Orb Spiders at Home!

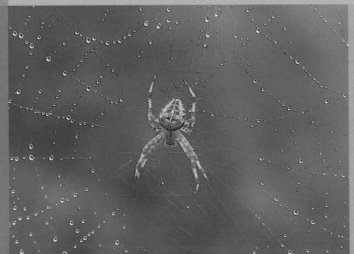

What a pretty web!
The spider uses its sticky web to catch food. A web is a nice, safe home for a spider.

Hello, Wolf Spider!

"That's one fuzzy spider, Piglet."
"I still don't think I want to pet it, Pooh."

Hatching and Growing!

These spiderlings are baby wolf spiders. They will ride on their mummy's back for a few days. Then they will be on their own.

Creeping, Crawling, and Flying

Go, go, go! Most spiders wait for food – such as a fly – to get stuck in their web. But not wolf spiders. They run after their dinner and catch it!

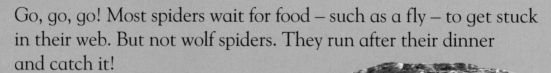

Wolf Spiders at Home!

What is down that hole? It's a wolf spider! Some wolf spiders dig little holes. Then they climb in and go to sleep.

Some butterflies taste things with their feet!

A Tigger prefers to use his tongue! Don't you?!

The Goliath beetle is the heaviest insect in the world.

It can weigh more than three ounces and grow as long as a brand-new pencil (six inches)!

Making a web is easy for a spider.

The orb spider can make a web in just one hour!

A Tigger's ears are on his head.

So are yours. But some crickets have sense organs on their *knees*.

THAT'S TIGGERIFIC!

Bees talk to one another by dancing.

A special dance lets other bees know where the tasty flowers are. Tiggers love to dance, too!

Tiggers are strong. Ants are, too.

An ant can carry something 20 times its size. That's like you carrying a horse!

Look and Find with Piglet!

Now you've learned about insects and spiders, look at the picture and answer the questions below.

- How many butterflies can you find?
- What has scared Piglet?
- What does Pooh have on his hand?
- Where is the caterpiller?
- How many grasshoppers can you find?
- What insect has stripes?
- How many wings does a dragonfly have?
- How many ants can you find?

INDEX

Photo credits
from left to right

Cover

Bios/Ruoso Hoaqui/Baccega Bios/OSF/Tyrell Hoaqui/Zefa Jacana/Cordier Jacana/Arndt Bios/Rotman Bios/Klein-Hubert Bios/von Schmieder Sunset/Holt Studio Bios/meul/Fotonatura
Title Page/copyright/introduction: Bios/Martin P 3: Hoaqui/Baccega Hoaqui/Zefa Jacana/Cordi

Chapter 1:

P 6: a) Bios/Denis-Huot b) Bios/Gunther c)Sunset/Lacz d)Jacana/Baccega P 7: a) Bios/Klein-Hubert b) Jacana/Shah c) Getty/Digital Vision P 8: a) Getty/DigitalVision
b) Getty/Stone/Monneret c) Getty/Taxi/Buss P 9: Sunset/Zephyr Images P 10: a) Phone/Gohier b) & c) Bios/Klein-Hubert P 11: Cogis/Lanceau P 12: a) Cogis/Français
b) Cogis/Gauzargues c) Cogis/Labat P 13: Cogis/Hermeline P 14: a) Colibri/Magnin b) Bios/Ruoso c) Sunset/Sunset P 15: Bios/Klein-Hubert P 16: a) Sunset/Holt Studio
b) Cogis/Lanceau c) Bios/Ruoso P 17: Bios/Gunther P 18: a) TapirBios/Heuclin b) Jacana/Hoaqui c) Jacana/PHR/Angermayer d) Colibri/Ermel P 19: a) Sunset/Horizon Vision
b) Bios/Pons P 20: a) Bios/Thouvenin b) Bios/Halleux c) Bios/Rocher P 21: Cogis/Labat P 22: a) Sunset/Visage b) Jacana/Danegger c) Bios/Leclerc P 23: Bios/Etienne
P 24: a) Sunset/Lacz b) Jacana/Walker c) Bios/Ausloos P 25: Bios/Klein-Hubert P 26: a) Sunset/Animals/Animals b) Sunset/Leeson c) Jacana/Lotscher P 27: Bios/Klein-Hubert
P 28: a) Bios/Denis-Huot b) Bios/Denis-Huot c) Bios/Nicolotti P 29: Colibri/Loubsens P 30: a) Sunset/German b) Bios/Day/OSF P 31: a) Bios/Klein-Hubert b) Bios/Ferrero/Labat
c) Bios/Bruemmer d) Bios/Ruoso P 32: a) Jacana/ Ph Researchers b) Colibri/Ratier c) Phone/Ferrero/Labat P 33: Sunset/Lacz P 34: a)Bios/Bonneau b)Hoaqui/Denis-Huot
c) Colibri/Haution P 35: Jacana/Pavard P 36: a) Colibri/Loubsens b) Jacana/Axel c) Bios/Valarcher P 37: Bios/Klein-Hubert 38: a) Sunset/Animals Animals b) Bios/Nicollotti
c) Bios/Denis-Huot P 39: Bios/Denis-Huot P 40: a) Jacana/Shah/Manoj b left & right) Bios/Ruoso c) Bios/Klein-Hubert P 41: Jacana/Shah/Manoj P 42: a) Getty/Images Bank/Schafer
b) Bios/Singh/OSF c) Bios/Montfort/Fotonatura P 43: a) Bios/Meinderts b) Bios/Denis-Huot c) Jacana/Pya P 44: a) Jacana/Baccega b) Hoaqui/Baccega c) Bios/Klein-Hubert
P 45: Phone/Valter P 46: a) Bios/Bahr b & c) Bios/Bruemmer P 47: Jacana/Durandal P 48: a & b) Sunset/Lacz c) Bios/Fotonatura/Visser P 49: Bios/Fotonatura/Visser
P 50: a & b) Getty/Images Bank/Su c) Getty/Images Bank/Vestal P 51: Bios/Schulz P 52: a & b) Bios/Ruoso c) Sunset/Lacz P 53: Bios/Ruoso

Chapter 2:

P 58: a)Bios/Seitre b) Sunset/West Stock c) Sunset/Horizon Vision P 59: a) Bios/Fève b) Hoaqui/Zefa Sunset c) Bios/Noto-CamPanella d) Sunset/Reinhard
P 60: a) Sunset/Guyon b & c) Sunset/FLPA P 61: Bios/Noto-Cam Panella P 61: a) Sunset/Mc Donald b) Sunset/Reinhard c) Sunset/Horizon Vision
P 62: a) Sunset/McDonald b) Sunset/Reinhard c) Sunset/Horizon Vision P 63: Bios/Alcalay P 64: a) Bios/Thiriet b) Bios/Ziesler c) Bios/Klein-Hubert P 65: Sunset/Horizon Vision
P 66: a) Bios/Sauvannet b) Bios/Seitre c) Bios/Tyrell P 67: Bios/OSF/Tyrell P 68: a) Bios/Gunther b) Bios/Seitre P 69: a) Bios/Robbrecht b) Sunset/Horizon Vision c) Sunset/Warde
d) Bios/Seitre e) Bios/Pernot P 70: a) Bios/Renaud b & c) Bios/Ruoso P 71: Bios/Fève P 72: a) Bios/Robert b) Bios/Gunther c) Bios/Granier P 73: Bios/Dennis P 73: Bios/Granier
P 74: a) Bios/Torterotot b & c) Sunset/Reinhard P 75: Sunset/Alaska Stock P 76: a) Sunset/Brake b) Bios/Seitre c) Sunset/Wolf P 77: Bios/Dragesco/Joffé P 78: a) Getty/Ston
b) Bios/Ruoso P 79: a) Getty/Stone/Gray b) Bios/Ziesler c) Bios/Puillandre d) Bios/Thouvenin P 80: a) Bios/Puillandre b) Sunset/Lacz c) Jacana/Ziesler
P 81: Sunset/West Stock P 82: a) Sunset /Kumar b) Bios/Wothe c) Sunset/Lacz P 83: Bios/Ziesler P 84: a) Sunset/Animals Animals b) Sunset/Leeson c) Sunset/McDonald
P 85: Sunset/Alaska Stock P 86: a) Bios/Fischer b) Sunset/Philipps c) Bios/Harvey P 87: Bios/Schulz b) Bios/Seitre c) Bios/Publiphoto/Schell

Chapter 3:

P 92: a) Jacana/Arndt b) AquaPress/Piednoir P 93: a) Bios/Ziegler b) AquaPress/Piednoir Sunset/Animals Animals c) Jacana/Arndt d) Sunset/Brake P 94: a) Bios/Bringard
b) Jacana/Cordier c) AquaPress/Piednoir P 95: Bios/Ziegler P 96: a & b) Bios/Gunther c) Sunset/Brake d) Bios/de La Harpe P 97: Bios/Gunther P 98: a) Bios/Bruemmer
b) Sunset/Levin c) Jacana/Scott P 99: AquaPress/Piednoir Sunset/Animals Animals P 100: a) Sunset/Animals Animals b) AquaPress/Piednoir c) Sunset/Hosking
P 101: AquaPress/Piednoir P 102: a) Bios/Gunther b) Sunset/Animals Animals c) Jacana/ChamProux d) Bios/Heuclin P 103: a) Bios/Halle/OSF b) Bios/Gunther
P 104: a) Jacana/Luquet b) Sunset/Animals Animals c) Jacana/Luquet P 105: Sunset/Lacz P 106: a & b Jacana/Arndt c) Hoaqui/Zefa P 107: Sunset/McDonald
P 108: a) Sunset/Ant b) Sunset/Lacz c) Sunset/Ant P 109: Bios/Ruoso P 110: a) Getty/Stone b) Bios/Maffart-Renaudier P 111: a) Bios/Pambour b) Sunset/Reinhard
c) Bios/Wattsd br: Getty/Taxi bl: Bios/Gunther P 112: a) Jacana/Dulhoste b) Jacana/Lanceau c) Sunset/Reinhard P 113: a) Sunset/Animals Animals b) Bios/Denis-Huot
c) Bios/Gayo P 114: a) AquaPress/Piednoir b) Bios/Heuclin c) Bios/Gayo P 115: Bios/Klein-Hubert P 116: a) Bios/Martin b) Jacana/Dulhoste c) Sunset/First Light
P 117: Sunset/German P 118: a) Sunset Levin b) Bios/Testu c) Sunset/Animals Animals P 119: Sunset/Animals Animals P 120: a) Bios/Heuclin
b) Bios/de La Harpe P 121: a) Sunset/Ant b) Bios/Heuclin c) Bios/Gayo

Chapter 4:

P 126: a) Sunset/Animals/Animals b)Sunset/JaPack c) Sunset /Lacz d) Bios/Denis-Huot P 127: a) Sunset/Perrine b)Sunset/Lacz c) Bios/Rotman/Arnold
P 128: a & b) Bios/Tavernier c) Sunset/JaPack P 129: AquaPress/Piednoir P 130: a-upper) Bios/Fournier, a-lower): Sunset/Lacz b) Sunset/Lacz c) Bios/Klein-Hubert P 131:
Sunset/Ant P 132: a) l Sunset/Perrin b) Bios/Fotonatura/Van Arkel c) Jacana/Winner P 133: Bios/Denis-Huot P 134: a) Bios/OSF/Kviter b) Bios/Tavernier c) Bios/Dirscherl
P 135: AquaPress/Piednoir P 136: a) Bios/Hall/OSF b) Bios/Rotmanxx P 137: a) Bios/Heuclin b) Bios/Tavernier c) Sunset/Animals Animals d) Bios/Tavernier/Nausicaa
P 138: a) Phone/Gohierb) Sunset/Perrine c) Jacana/Amsler P 139: Jacana/PhResearchers/Faulkner P 140: a) Jacana/Winner b) Jacana/Wu c) AquaPress/Piednoir
P 141: AquaPress/Piednoir P 142: a) Sunset/FLPA b) AquaPress/Piednoir Bios/Rotman c) Bios/Gilson P 143: Phone/Danna P 144: a) Sunset/Perrine b) Jacana/Gladu c) Jacana/Amsler
P 145: Sunset/Lacz P 146: a) AquaPress/Piednoir b) Getty/Taxi/Docwhite P 147: a) ul : Phone/Goetgheluck b) ur : Sunset/Lacz c) Jacana/PhResearchers/Westmorland
d) Bios/Klein-Hubert P 148: a) Bios/OkaPia/Stevens b) Getty/Stone/Krebsc) Sunset/Lacz P 149: Sunset/Lacz P 150: a) Sunset/FLPA b) Bios/Bavendam c) Bios/Pacorel
P 151: Sunset/Animals Animals P 152: a) Bios/Tavernier b) Sunset/Pakiela c) Bios/Tavernier c) Bios/Delobelle P 153: Bios/Hill/OSF P 154: a) Bios/Gautier
b) Bios/Tavernierc) Bios/Henno/Wildlife P 155: a) Bios/Seitre b) Bios/Bavendam c) Bios/Rotman

Chapter 5:

P 160: a)Bios/Martin b)Sunset/Bringard c)Bios/Da Cunha P 161: a) Sunset/Lorne b) Bios/Gayo c) Jacana/PHR P 162: a) Bios/Bringard a) Sunset/FLPA b) Jacana/PHR
c) Sunset/Gallo Images P 163: Sunset/Bringard P 164: a) Sunset/NHPA b) Bios/Da Cunha c) Bios/Fotonatura/Meul P 165: Bios/Da Cunha P 166: a) Sunset/Lorne
b) Bios/Fotonatura/van Arkel c) Jacana/Lorne P 167: Bios/Bringard P 168: a) Bios/Frebet b) Bios/Heras c) Bios/Fotonatura/Meul P 169: Bios/Gayo P 170: a) Sunset/Animals Animals
b) Jacana/Moiton c) Bios/Martin P 171: a) Jacana/Lorne b) Bios/von Schmiederc) Sunset/NHPA P 172: a) Bios/Bahr b) Bios/Etienne
c) Bios/Vincent P 173: Bios/OkaPia/Reinhard P 174: a) Bios/Bertani b & c) Bios/Martin d) Jacana/Arndt P 175 : Bios/Fisher P 176: a) Sunset/Animals Animals b) Sunset/Prevot
c) Bios/Borel P 177: Sunset/Prevot P 178: a-upper) Sunset/FLPA, a-lower) Sunset/Prevot b) Bios/Labhardt c) Jacana/Boccaletti P 179: Bios/Bringard P 180: a) Bios/Bringard
b) Getty/taxi/Du Feu c) Sunset/Delfino P 181: a) Bios/Denis-Huot b) Sunset/Holt Studio c) Sunset/NHPA P 182: a) Getty/Images Bank/Carmichael b) Getty/Stone/Davies&Starr
c) Sunset/Holt Studio P 183: a) Getty/Images Bank/Carmichael b) Getty/Stone/Davies & Starr c)Bios/Vincent P 184: a) Bios/Pfletschinger b) Bios/Pfletschinger
c) Bios/Gomes P 185: Bios/Vincent P 186: a) Jacana/Larivière b) Sunset/Holt Studio c) Sunset/Lorne P 187: Sunset/McDonald
P 188: a) Bios/Bringard b) Bios/Fagot c) Bios/Gunther d) Bios/Gayo P 189: a) Bios/OSF/Dennis b) Bios/Bringard

Index: Bios/Martin Bios/Von Schmieder Bios/Gunther Bios/Klein-Hubert Phone/Goetgheluck Sunset/Lacz Bios/Tavernier Bios/PubliPhoto/SchellBios/Rotman Sunset/FLPA

The following people have collaborated in the making of this book.
Sylvie Basdevant-Suzuki , Jim Breheny, Nathalie Cagnat, April Dahlberg, Eric Elzière Audrey Fallope, François Guion